CLASSIC ROCK FOR TWO

T0082039

Arrangements by Peter Deneff

ISBN 978-1-5400-6543-8

Visit Hal Leonard Online at
www.halleonard.com

Contact Us:
Hal Leonard
7777 West Bluemound Road
Milwaukee, WI 53213
Email: info@halleonard.com

In Europe contact:
Hal Leonard Europe Limited
42 Wigmore Street
Marylebone, London, W1U 2RN
Email: info@halleonardeurope.com

In Australia contact:
Hal Leonard Australia Pty. Ltd.
4 Lentara Court
Cheltenham, Victoria, 3192 Australia
Email: info@halleonard.com.au

BANG A GONG
(Get It On)

TRUMPETS

Words and Music by
MARC BOLAN

Medium Rock

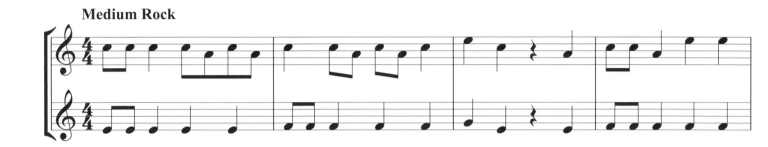

CAN'T FIGHT THIS FEELING

TRUMPETS

Words and Music by
KEVIN CRONIN

Rock Ballad

CARRY ON WAYWARD SON

TRUMPETS

Words and Music by
KERRY LIVGREN

Moderate Rock

COLD AS ICE

TRUMPETS

Words and Music by MICK JONES
and LOU GRAMM

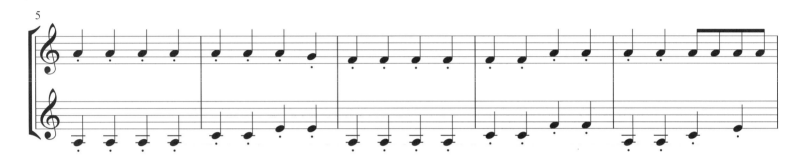

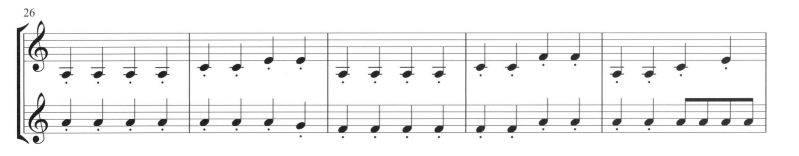

COME ON EILEEN

Words and Music by KEVIN ROWLAND,
JAMES PATTERSON and KEVIN ADAMS

TRUMPETS

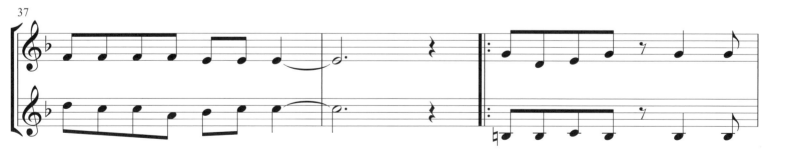

COME TOGETHER

TRUMPETS

Words and Music by JOHN LENNON
and PAUL McCARTNEY

Moderately

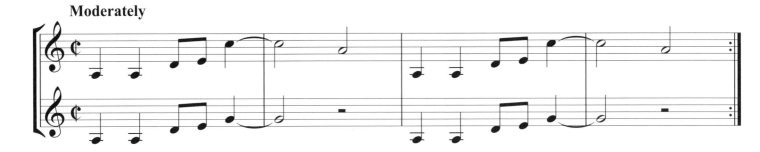

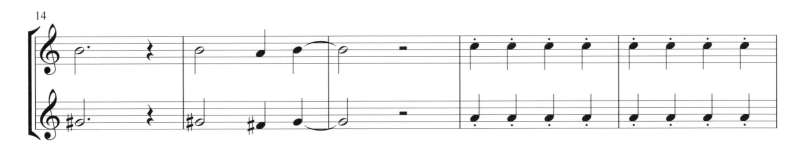

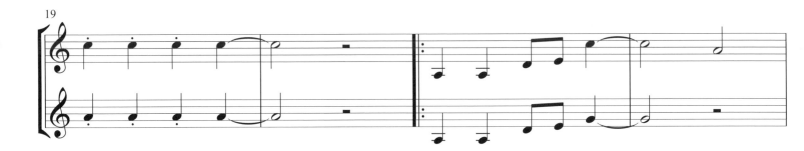

CROCODILE ROCK

TRUMPETS

Words and Music by ELTON JOHN
and BERNIE TAUPIN

Lively

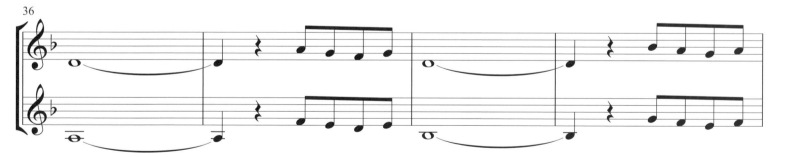

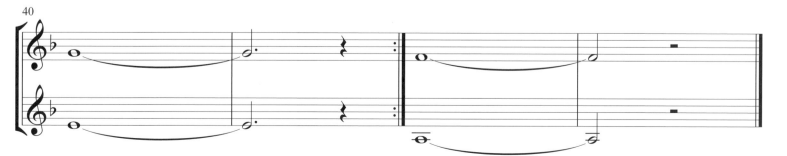

DOWN ON THE CORNER

TRUMPETS

Words and Music by
JOHN FOGERTY

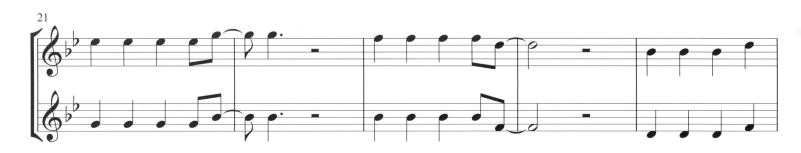

EVERY LITTLE THING SHE DOES IS MAGIC

TRUMPETS

Words and Music by
STING

Moderately fast

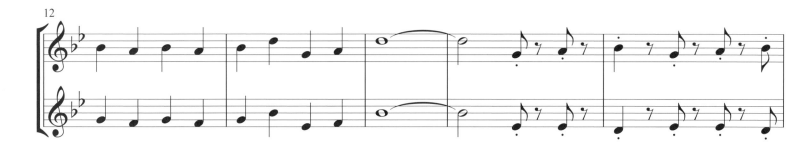

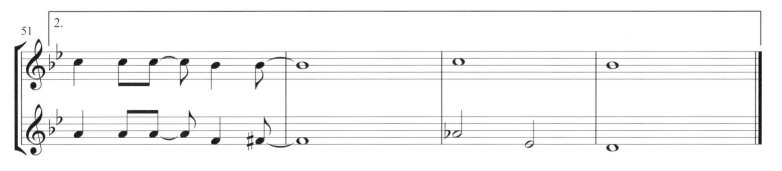

FREE FALLIN'

TRUMPETS

Words and Music by TOM PETTY
and JEFF LYNNE

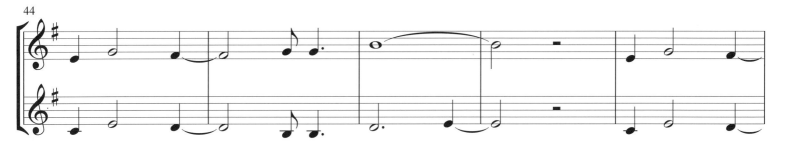

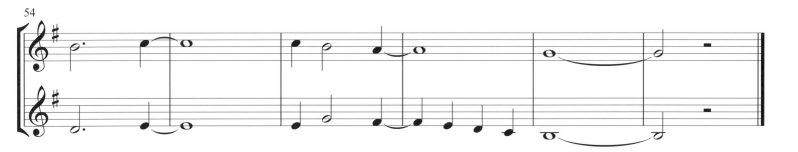

HURTS SO GOOD

TRUMPETS

Words and Music by JOHN MELLENCAMP
and GEORGE GREEN

Moderate Rock

To Coda ⊕

CODA
⊕

D.S. al Coda

THE JOKER

TRUMPETS

Words and Music by STEVE MILLER,
EDDIE CURTIS and AHMET ERTEGUN

Moderately

LIVIN' ON A PRAYER

TRUMPETS

Words and Music by JON BON JOVI,
DESMOND CHILD and RICHIE SAMBORA

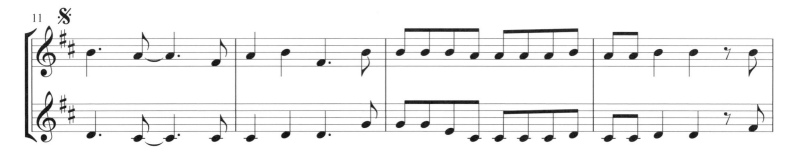

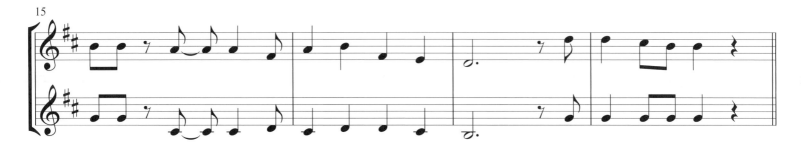

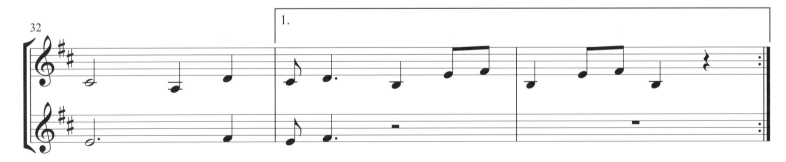

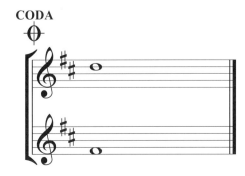

MAGGIE MAY

TRUMPETS

Words and Music by ROD STEWART
and MARTIN QUITTENTON

Moderately

MR. ROBOTO

TRUMPETS

Words and Music by
DENNIS DeYOUNG

Play 3 times

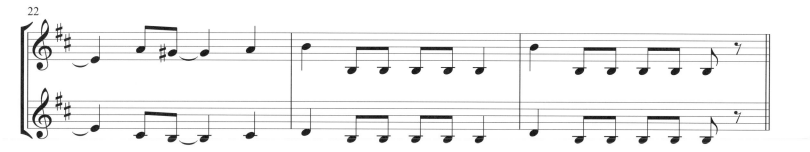

MONEY FOR NOTHING

TRUMPETS

Words and Music by MARK KNOPFLER
and STING

Moderate Rock

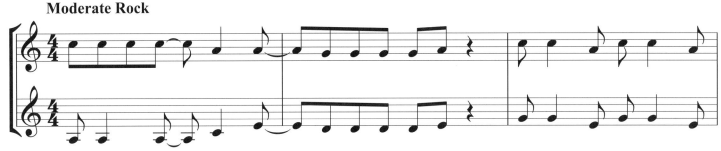

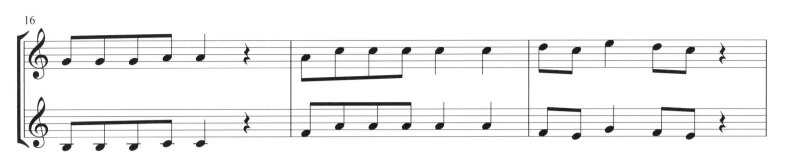

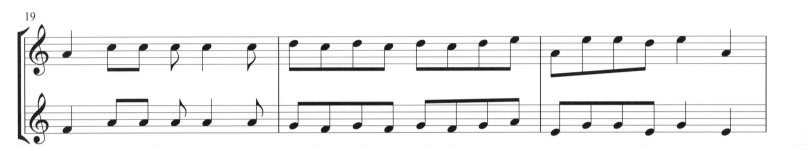

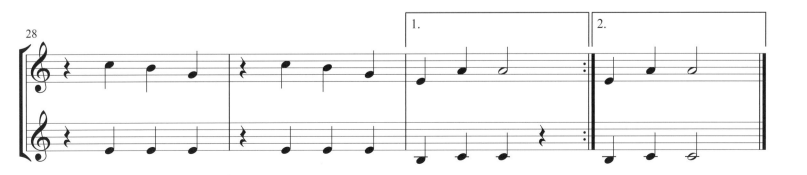

ONE MORE NIGHT

TRUMPETS

Words and Music by
PHIL COLLINS

Moderate Ballad

PEACE OF MIND

TRUMPETS

Words and Music by
TOM SCHOLZ

REELING IN THE YEARS

TRUMPETS

Words and Music by WALTER BECKER
and DONALD FAGEN

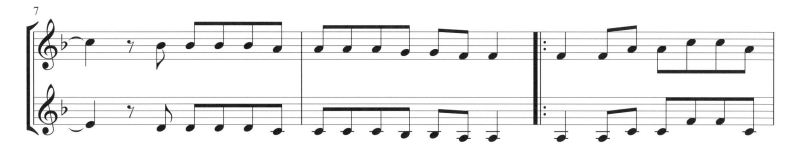

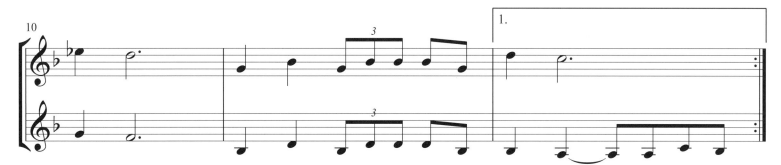

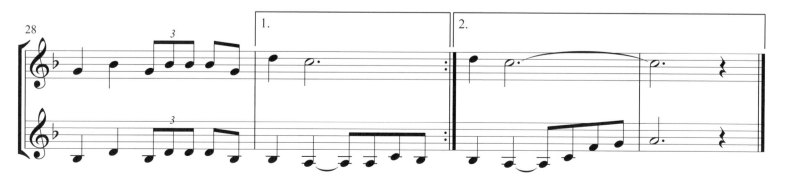

SMOKE ON THE WATER

TRUMPETS

Words and Music by RITCHIE BLACKMORE,
IAN GILLAN, ROGER GLOVER,
JON LORD and IAN PAICE

Moderate Rock

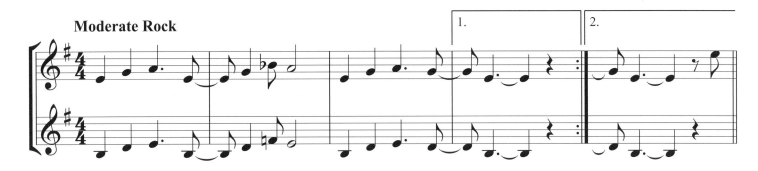

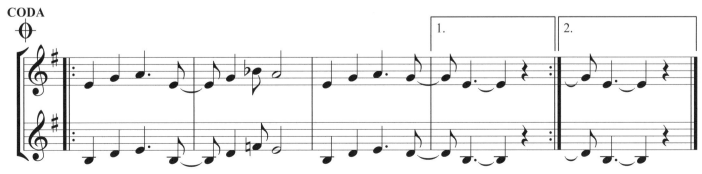

SUMMER OF '69

TRUMPETS

Words and Music by BRYAN ADAMS
and JIM VALLANCE

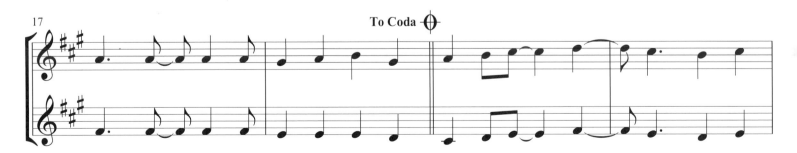

D.C. al Coda

CODA

UPTOWN GIRL

TRUMPETS

Words and Music by
BILLY JOEL

Moderately

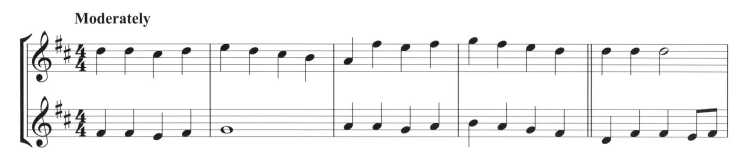

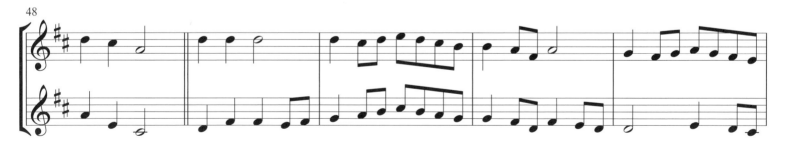

YOU'RE THE INSPIRATION

TRUMPETS

Words and Music by PETER CETERA
and DAVID FOSTER

Rock Ballad

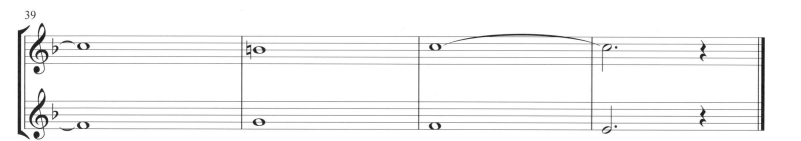